ORCA SONG

SMITHSONIAN OCEANIC COLLECTION

For Tara, who reminded me
how difficult it is to allow what is natural
and shy of civilization to remain so.
　—M.A.

To Morgan
　—K.L.

ISBN 0-590-35719-0

12 11 10 9 8 7 6 5 4 3 2 1   7 8 9/9 0 1 2/0

Printed in the U.S.A.   08
First Scholastic printing, November 1997

ORCA SONG

by **Michael C. Armour**   Illustrated by **Katie Lee**

SCHOLASTIC INC.
New York Toronto London Auckland Sydney

A rosy sun settles over the sea. A dusk wind dances up the waves. The moon climbs out of the Olympic Mountains. And eight Orca whales come leaping up the Washington coast.

Stories are told that 50 million years ago, ancestors of the Orca whale walked upon the land on all fours. But they so loved the water they gave up their hands and legs to have fins and tail flukes. Now Orca is the greatest and most powerful hunter in all the oceans of the world.

The leader of the pod, Bull Orca, echolocates. By sending vibrating sounds through the water, he can locate and tell the nature of objects far beyond his sight. He finds a school of salmon circling within fishermen's nets. It is a familiar practice — the whole pod will slip into the nets to feed, then escape before the fishermen notice.

Splashing and singing at the rear of the group, not at all like a hunter, is Orca the Pup. Bull Orca suddenly turns the pod toward the nets. He and the herd speed to the noisy, splashing salmon.

Just at that moment, Pup turns the opposite way — toward a juicy salmon nearby.

As Pup's great jaws open to snatch his catch, a storm of fishing boats close in on the whales. Bull Orca wheels around and the pod races for safety. Pup moves to join them.

But he can't! His dorsal fin is caught in a sunken, abandoned cargo net.

Pup wriggles and squirms. He bucks and thrashes. The net only gets tighter. Then he lies still, nearly out of breath, too weak to call out.

Above him, the rumbling of the boats grows fainter as they move away. Pup hears his mother calling him. He is only five, and has never been more than a hundred yards from her side. But her voice, like the others, soon fades.

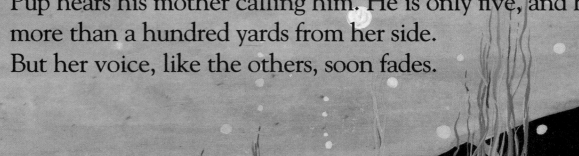

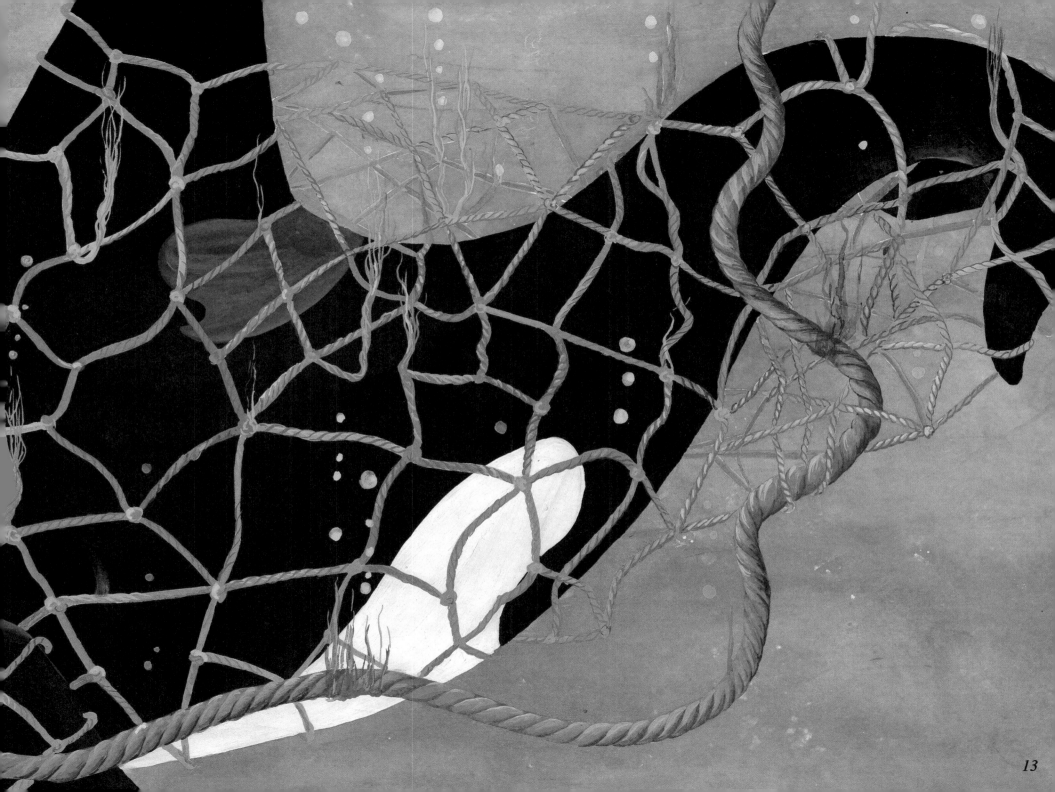

13

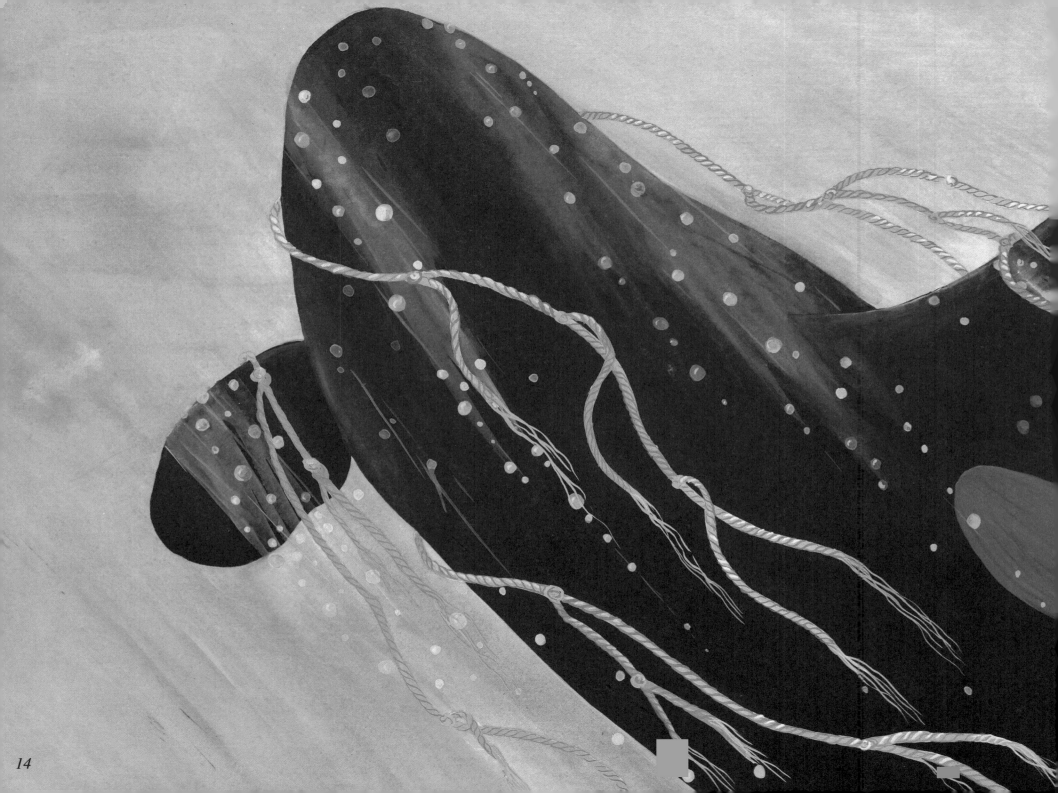

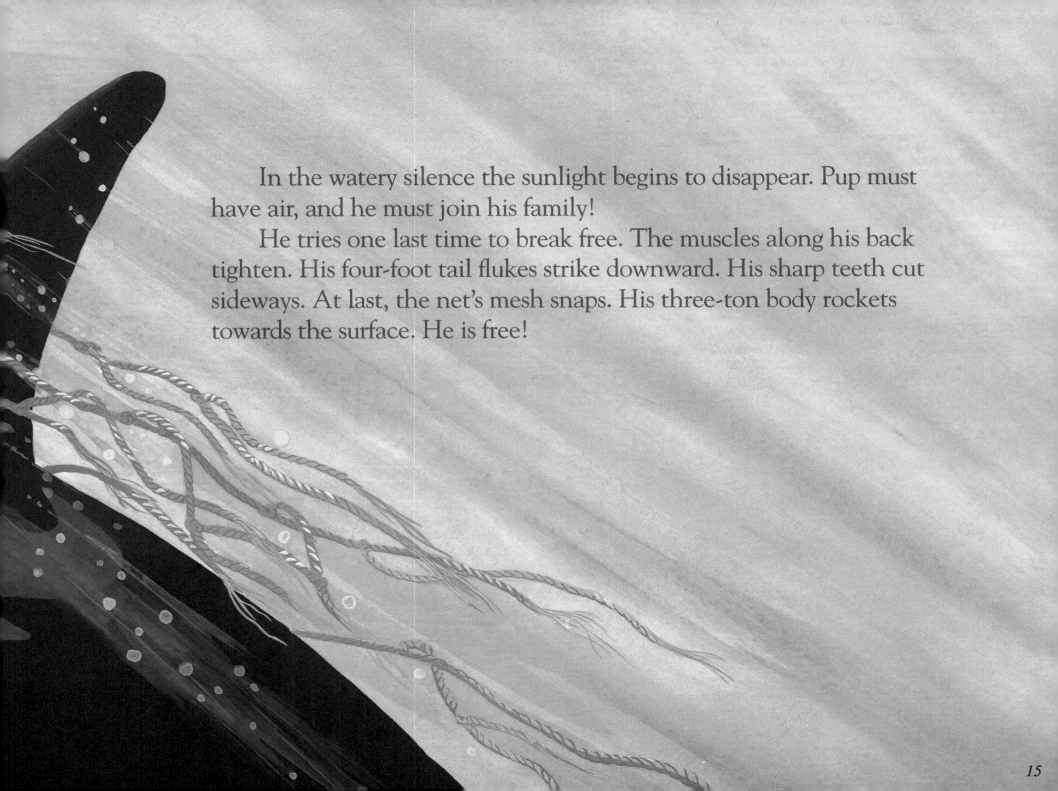

In the watery silence the sunlight begins to disappear. Pup must have air, and he must join his family!

He tries one last time to break free. The muscles along his back tighten. His four-foot tail flukes strike downward. His sharp teeth cut sideways. At last, the net's mesh snaps. His three-ton body rockets towards the surface. He is free!

Air! Night air rushes into his blowhole. His lungs fill like balloons.
But the fight has tired him. Alone and exhausted, Pup drifts,
half-asleep, through the lonely, moonlit seas...closer and closer to land.

From the shadowy hills nearby, ancient totem poles rise up to the stars. For centuries the Native Americans along the western coast carved totems that celebrated Orca's brave hunting skills.

But, unseen by Pup, the totems slide by as the moon goes out of the sky.

Dawn breaks. Pup awakes, feeling the sun's growing heat on his back. Unaware, he had drifted toward the shore and became stuck in a shallow pool of water. The waves must have pushed him here in the night.

The outgoing tide has left a sandbar between him and the sea where he belongs. No whale can endure so much direct sun, and the sun is still rising!

Pup has grown to understand the meanings of many sounds in the sea. Yet surrounding him now are strange voices.

Along his back he feels many soft tickling sensations. Suddenly he is being moved. Something is pushing him through the rising water of the incoming tide. Pushing him back to the sea. Back to the cold. Back to life!

23

He takes a grateful gulp of air and dives — down past the
dark underwater caverns — down past the fluttering kelp beds.
The cold water cools his body.

Pup begins to echolocate. He finds a school
of herring and races for it.

But Pup is young and inexperienced.
All the fish hear him coming and scatter.

Still alone and looking for his family, Pup sees three humpback whales rise up out of the hidden valleys of the undersea. Their slow whistling songs are different than the songs his family uses.

But within the notes, as if from a far-off world, Pup hears another, more urgent song, an Orca song.

Pup turns and drives his sleek body toward the surface.
He breaks out of the water in a sky-bound spiral! He lands
with a tail-whopping splash that can be heard clear to the mountains
of the Olympic Peninsula.

He looks for signs — a fin, a fluke — any signs, along the coast.

And then, silhouetted against the sunset, Pup sees them — seven whales, his very own family, rising out of the waves, coming for him. They have not left him! They have come back!

Their songs of happiness race before them like ribbons of joy. Orca the Pup is home again.

About the Orca Whale

The Orca whale, also called "killer whale", has no natural enemies, apart from humans. Weighing four to ten tons, these warm blooded, air-breathing mammals grow to 30 feet long and may live as long as 50 years.

Young Orca pups are bound by life-long ties to their mothers, usually swimming no more than 100 yards from their sides. Orcas often travel in pods over long distances to feed on the seasonal food supplies. Generally, young Orcas play together, and, by their teens, their bodies are covered with scars from boisterous years.

Orcas are best known for their distinctive jumping and swimming abilities. Besides speeding and turning easily underwater, Orcas perform acrobatic feats above water, such as spy hops, flipper slaps, belly whops, spiralling breaches and barrel rolls.

Glossary

dorsal fin: The fin on an Orca's back.

echolocate: To locate an object in the water through a series of high energy clicking sounds emitted from an Orca's blowhole. These sounds bounce off an object and echo back to the Orca, revealing the object's size, shape and location.

fluke: The flat part of an Orca's tail.

kelp: Any of a variety of large brown seaweed.

pod: A group of whales, generally from the same family, that swim together.

sandbar: A bank of sand built up from the water close to the shoreline.

tide: The rising and falling of the ocean, occurring twice a day.

totem poles: Carved wooden sculptures erected by Native Americans to commemorate various animals or people.

Points of Interest in this Book

pp. 4-5 sea gulls, lob-tailing (slapping tail flukes on the surface of the water).

pp. 6-7, 8-9 purse seine nets.

pp. 6-7, 8-9, 10-11 chinook salmon.

pp. 24-25 kelp, Pacific herring.

pp. 26-27 humpback whales.

pp. 28-29 breaching (an Orca breaking the water's surface completely).

pp. 30-31 spyhopping (an Orca seemingly standing vertically in the water with one half or more of its body surfaced).